Rockin' Out With Blues Fiddle

By Julie Lyonn Lieberman

Julie Lyonn Music
Distributed by Hal Leonard

JD

Dedication and Acknowledgments

This book is dedicated to my father, sculptor and writer Ben Lieberman. Dad listened to me back in 1976 in my Uncle Robert's favorite Chinese restaurant at 84th and Broadway as I described my plans to write this book. He offered me the same patient support he'd sustained through my teenage years when, night after night, after a long work day, he'd sit at the kitchen table teaching me how to write by asking questions and encouraging me to let go of favorite phrases in favor of clear communication.

This is the fifth edition of *Rockin' out with Blues Fiddle*. The book has changed enormously with each stage of its journey. I was originally encouraged to write it by Jason Shulman of Oak Publications, but the first edition was actually published by Mel Bay Publications through the support of Bill Bay. The third edition was created for publication with Music Sales (parent company to Oak Publications). Blues collectors Robert Javors, Chris Strachwitz, Pete Lowry, Sheldon Harris, and Bob Koester all gave generously of their time and expertise in its early stages. Editors Henry Rasof, Melissa Stielman, and Leonard Vogler also contributed to the book's first installments.

Now, at last, I hope this is its final journey into completed form. Perhaps it couldn't really find its final and lasting format until it was complete with backing tracks on iTunes and reshaped by an author who's now been teaching and performing this material for many, many decades. [www.JulieLyonn.com]

Cover Design: Loren Moss

Photo Credits:
Many thanks to Russ Dantzler for the photo of Claude Williams; to Susan Ruel for her photo of Clarence Gatemouth Brown; to Marshall Wyatt for his amazing photos of Will Batts, the Mobile Strugglers, and the Armstrong Family; to Randy Resnick and Jack Terry Music for the photos of Sugarcane Harris; and to The Howard Armstrong Collection as well as American Legends for the use of their photo of Howard Armstrong.

Copyright ©2022 Julie Lyonn Music
Worthington, MA

Lieberman, Julie Lyonn
Rockin' Out with Blues Fiddle

Bibliography.
Includes index.
1. Blues Violin 2. Strings 3. Rock Violin 4. String Improvisation
5. Blues Fiddle 6. Violin 7. Fiddle

Exclusive Distributor:
Hal Leonard Corporation (music stores)
ISBN: 978-1-879730-11-3

TABLE OF CONTENTS

INTRODUCTION

The blues is an incredibly expressive form of music. Predecessor to R&B and rock, its basic 12-bar 3-chord form creates an environment within which you, the soloist, have room to exercise a wide range of creative choices.

Whether your style embraces elegantly simple lines tailored to the blues scale or chords; gutsy, soulfully wrenching passages; sophisticated bebop lines; highly textured figures; or bold explorations that move way outside the key before tucking the phrase neatly back in; the blues welcomes it all. Since the violin is capable of bending notes, sliding in and out of pitch, moaning, whispering, and more, it is one of the closest instruments to the human voice that we have.

This book is designed to provide you with all of the tools you will need to play well in a blues or rock/pop setting. If you're new to this style, you will find that learning the blues will activate your imagination: your right- and left-hand touch will change in sometimes obvious but often subtle ways, and you will be called upon to transition from the role of anonymous interpretive artist to one of creating an individual presence on your instrument.

BACKING TRACKS AVAILABLE ON ITUNES ...

Watch for this symbol to coordinate the tracks with the book.

Track One will give you an "A" to tune to.

Violin: Julie Lyonn Lieberman
Guitar: Matt Munisteri
Bass: Steve Alcott
Drums: Owen Howard
Engineer: Eve Seltzer
Recorded at Passport Studio, New York, NY

A Blue Odyssey Into Fiddling

Blues Styles

There are two types of blues: **country blues** and **jazz blues.** The first blues form to evolve was a simpler form. Country blues developed in rural areas of the South. Originally there were many variations, such as one-chord blues, or odd numbers of measures like eleven-bar or thirteen-bar blues. At that time, greater importance was placed on the emotional content of the lyrics and the vocal style than on adhering to a rigid form. It was primarily a vocal music first, which gradually transferred first to violin, then other instruments. Eventually, the form solidified into a twelve-bar, three-chord form using the I, IV, and V chords of the key for accompaniment. For instance, if the song was in the key of G, the first chord was a G7, followed by a chord built on the fourth of its key, C7, then D7 and back home.

In the early days, country blues was usually performed by a solo singer accompanying himself on guitar. If he played in a band, the group would generally include a blues fiddler and a second guitarist or mandolin player. Terms like Delta blues, Texas blues, Mississippi blues, or Chicago blues, evolved over time to describe different rhythmic grooves used for the accompaniment as well as the point of origin and traits that developed regionally.

Drums and piano were added when the blues came to the city (**urban blues**) and later, the instruments were amplified to project over noise in bars. The predecessor to rock and roll, R&B (rhythm and blues), used a big-voiced belting style and added piano, bass, and drums into the rhythm section, making the music highly danceable. All these variations honored that same twelve-bar form, except some bands used more chords than the traditional three.

Built on the twelve-bar form, the chord changes in **jazz blues** are more complicated than the simple I IV V of the country blues. A rhythm section is used, and it is common to hear this music played on saxophone, trumpet, and other instruments associated with jazz.

Each chord conveys the tonal center for the scale you choose to use and its accompanying symbol describes the notes of its scale.

This 12-bar form, due its high level of repetition and emphasis on the tonal center (the key signature) provides a scaffold over which you can play expressively using very few notes, or overlay more and more complex ideas based on chord substitutions—more on that later.

If you aren't familiar with how to improvise over chords, you can get started using the notes of any of the following three scales per the key signature and ignore the other chords.

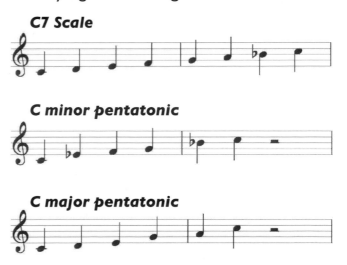

C7 Scale

C minor pentatonic

C major pentatonic

Then layer in skills step-by-step by mastering the scales for the other two (or more chords(. Use the first two accompaniments on the CD to practice outlining your chord tones and scales.

The keys on the backing tracks are B, since guitarists are most at ease in the keys of E and B, and Bb to prepare to play with jazz instruments. But you can use an app to transpose those backing tracks into whatever key you want to play in. My professional students learn to play the blues in all twelve keys since singers don't care if a key is challenging for the members of the band. They'll choose to sing in whatever key suits their vocal range!

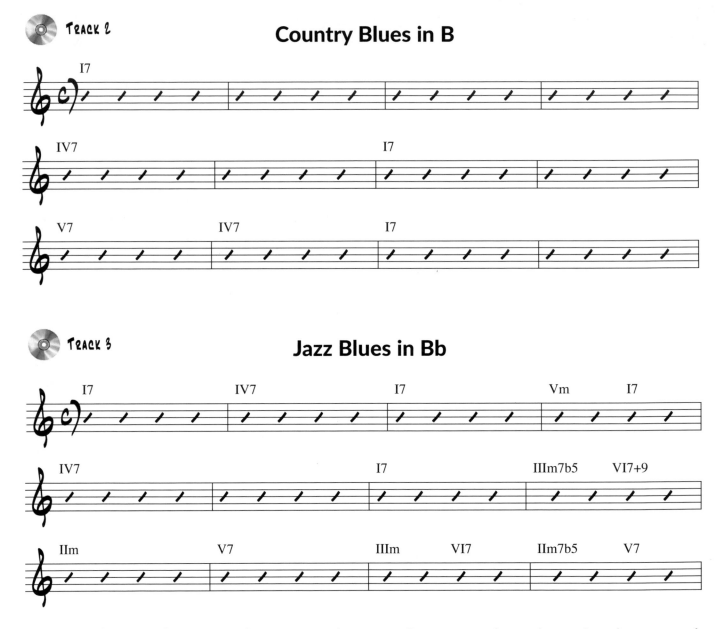

TRACK 2

Country Blues in B

TRACK 3

Jazz Blues in Bb

You may be wondering, at this point, why Roman numerals and not the names of the chords, i.e. B7, E7, and F#7 to describe the chords. This is because once you master the structure, it becomes easier to:

• Recognize the relationship between the chords (up a fourth or fifth from the root note).

• Lock the harmonic motion into your ears,.

• Jam with other musicians with ease, particularly if they call off a song in a key you haven't practiced before.

Basics for Blues Improvisation

In blues or jazz, the key signature only defines the seven scale tones appropriate to use while playing the melody. Once you start to improvise, the notes you use will come from the chords. Each time a new chord appears in the music, you can use the chord tones (1, 3, 5, ♭7) of the key and the chordal scale the symbol represents. In the blues, the dominant seventh chord is the most popular chord. It uses a major scale with a flatted seventh:

Blues is an interesting cross between a modal (one scale) and harmonic (chord progression) approach to improvisation. Jazz blues, of course is more complex.

Learning the blues is a much gentler approach to improvisation for the novice. You can create a valid and even interesting improvisation using just one or two notes played expressively with spicy rhythms.

You may be wondering, at this point, why bother to learn the chords if I can solo using the three scales—major scale with a flatted seventh or one of the two pentatonic scales—in the key of the tune. It's expected that you will solo for more than one *chorus*. The word *chorus* describes the full form. A blues chorus lasts 12 measures (or bars), a swing tune lasts 32 bars, and so on.

If you only use one or two scales, your ideas will tend to become highly repetitive. The more spice you can add, the longer you will hold interest ... whether your own, your bandmates, or audience.

A few pages back, I mentioned *chord substitutions*. Basically, it comes down to this: You can use any notes you want, in any order, as long as your ears say "yes." But if you master more advanced

chordal scales, you'll be able to audiate (hear in your mind) and physically capture what you hear in more and more interesting ways.

There are at least four primary chord types and each describes a different kind of scale that can be used in addition to the dominant seventh chordal scale and the two pentatonic scales. (For more information, see my books *Improvising Violin* or *The Contemporary Violinist*.)

To deepen your options, be sure to practice the chord tones as diligently as you practice the scales. When translating these examples to other keys, learn the degrees of the scale first, and then apply to the key of your choice.

B♭ minor:

B♭m7♭5:

B♭ altered:

B♭ diminished:

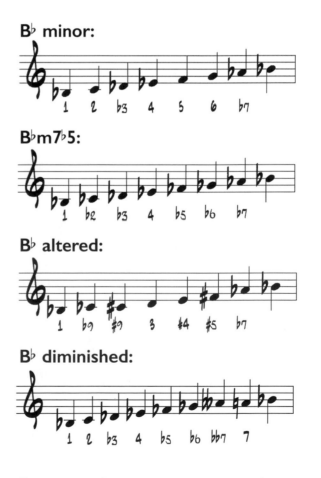

For extra spice, you can even superimpose snippets of an augmented scale or arpeggio:

chord tones: 1 3 ♯5 ♭7

scale tones: 1 2 3 ♯4 ♯5 ♭7

Whole-Brain Thinking

Unlike keyboard players and guitarists, violinists tend to think one note at a time. This approach isn't useful when it comes to playing over chord changes. And if you've been trained to rely on reading music for the source of what you play, you will have to retrain your brain.

Those of us fortunate enough to learn melodies by ear, tend to play folk styles where the melody is repeated over and over with slight changes through ornamentation, and there is little or no opportunity to improvise (unless on one or two scales).

When playing the blues, you will have the opportunity to develop and call upon new mental skills.

1) You will develop the ability to access a whole-brain balance between analytical (left-brain) and creative (right-brain) thinking which will enable you to track the chord changes and their appropriate chordal scales in the order they appear in the tune while improvising;

2) You will develop imagistic (right-brain) thinking which will enable you to picture all twelve keys—shaped to whatever type of scale is needed— across the instrument as a multi-dimensional map.

3) You will access your creativity (right-brain) as you develop your improvisatory skills, and,

4) You will cultivate deep listening skills in order to remember what you've already played while audiating (hearing inside your head) the line you're about to create.

Assume it's going to take you at least a couple of years to assimilate this new mental balance, depending upon your level of technique and flexibility. Learning to create new sounds on your instrument will require a shift in how you coordinate both hands in order to transition from a classical or fiddle sound into playing the blues. High levels of technique don't always mean faster access, because the sounds of whichever styles you've spent years mastering get built into muscle memory, and it will take time to learn how to sound bluesy.

Learning the Keys

Learning your twelve key signatures and twelve major scales is well worth the time as a preparation for flatting your sevenths for the blues, and for learning to play the blues in all twelve keys:

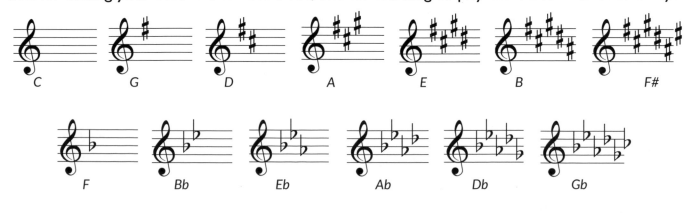

BLUES FIDDLE TECHNIQUE

There are certain left- and right-hand techniques that are synonymous with a bluesy sound on violin. These same techniques can be applied when playing rock/pop. Once you are familiar with these techniques and understand the basic harmonic foundation of the blues, you will find it easy to apply this information to different keys and blues forms.

Listening is essential to learning any genre. As you absorb the information in this book, and more particularly in this chapter, try to listen to as many different interpretations of the blues as possible. Keep in mind that the vocal style came first, and it's essential to listen to and mirror vocals sounds on your instrument.

Take in the incredible sounds of Leadbelly, B.B. King, Muddy Waters, Lonnie Johnson, and Son House, to name but a few of the many incredible artists who have made major contributions to the blues. It is equally important to place yourself in as many playing situations as possible. As avant garde jazz violinist Leroy Jenkins said to me in interview, "You can study forever, but the real learning happens out on the field." Everyone must overcome fear, embarrassment, feelings of inadequacy or whatever else comes up around getting together with other musicians to jam. Many of us experience outright humiliation as we slip and slide all over the instrument "trying to find it;" but nothing replaces experience!

Blues Vibrato

Vibrato can be used quite effectively in the blues, but not classical vibrato, which tends to be consistent and too pretty. In the blues context, think of vibrato as one of many ways you can add color to your notes. Variations in vibrato are achieved through control of the

width and **speed** of your finger motion. Sometimes you may choose to play a whole passage with an evenly rolled vibrato; other times you may avoid vibrato altogether until reaching a phrase or note that you wish to accentuate. You can change your vibrato on one note by starting out slow and wide and then gradually picking up speed and narrowing the width. There are moments when a wide, hysterical vibrato may suit the musical phrase.

Develop control over vibrato by practicing rolling slightly below and up to the pitch at different speeds. This often easier in second position with your second finger on an E on the A string.

Lean finger a quarter tone flat and back to pitch to pitch, or slide finger pitch to pitch:

TRACK 4

Blues Slides

There are a number of different ways to slide into a pitch. Slides are hard to notate as is evidenced by the East Indian tradition which teaches hundreds of glissando techniques through apprenticeship rather than notation. Slides can be used to create many different effects. You can vary the speed of the finger motion, the distance traveled, and how you accentuate that action with your bow. It is essential to keep your left thumb as relaxed as possible and finger pressure at a minimum.

The following examples are based on the styles of several specific players and represent only a few of the possibilities available to you. This first example illustrates Nap Hayes' slide technique. He would head towards a specific pitch a sixteenth note early, reaching it at just the crucial moment:

In addition to small subtle slides either in or out of pitch, you can also slide a larger distance by moving from one pitch to another the way Eddie Anthony did when he played:

Lonnie Johnson had a way of either rolling or sliding his fingertip up and down, achieving two completely different sounds:

Jazz violinist Joe Kennedy, Jr. sometimes used a chromatic slide technique:

Blues Tremolo or Shimmer

The classical term *tremolo* indicates a fast, symmetrical up-and-down movement at the tip of the bow. For instance, Will Batts sometimes used tremolo to kick off his solos. I use the term "shimmer" to indicate a bow motion too fast and too small to measure. Rather than an evenly measured stroke, it becomes a texture.

Some players, like Howard Armstrong, trilled or bent notes with their left hand, while shimmering them with the bow.

If you are not familiar with this bow technique, keep your wrist loose but not floppy and let the impulse come from your forearm. The movement should consist of a very fast up-and-down motion using less than half an inch of hair at the tip of the bow.

Blues Meter and Rhythm

Almost every song in this book is in 4/4. There are some jazz composers (Miles Davis and Wes Montgomery, among others) who have composed blues tunes in 3/4 or 6/8 time, but 4/4 is the most common meter you'll ever come across in the blues.

The blues is empowered by the use of syncopated rhythms, which provide an element of tension and surprise. Syncopation shifts the accent from the strong part of the beat to the weak part of the beat. For instance:

Here is an example of syncopation typical of Carl Martin's handiwork:

Blues Harmonic Structure

The tunes in this book are in the standard twelve-bar blues country blues form with only the I7 IV7 V7 progression we discussed earlier. The I IV V are all derived in relationship to the key signature. For instance, if the key signature tells you that you are in the key of Bb, then you will use the Bb7 (I), Eb7 (IV), and F7 (V) chords for your twelve-bar chord progression.

TRACK 6

Optional Scales

The blues progression is so dependable and repetitious, that eventually the player can superimpose snippets of other types of scales over the dominant seventh chord. This should only be attempted when you know where you are at all times and have mastered your dominant seventh scales, blue notes (the addition of the flatted 3rd and 5th) as well as the minor

and major pentatonic scales. The diminished or whole tone scale can be used as long as you return to a primary chord tone or the regular scale to end your phrase.

My approach is to balance journeys outside the traditional chordal scales with dissonant ideas and chord substitutions discussed earlier in this book. But I always "tuck back in" to whatever chord the band is playing. This requires an indelible imprint of the twelve-bar time increment..

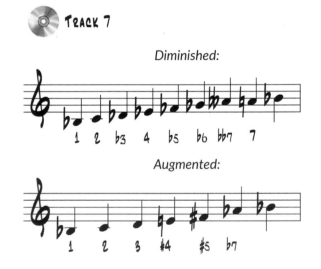

TRACK 7

Glossary of Scales

On the following three pages I have provided you with dominant seventh chordal scales with "blue notes" (b3 and b5), and pentatonic (five-note) scales in all twelve keys. These three forms of scale can be used during improvisation. The more adept you become at incorporating them into your solos, the more patterns and pitch possibilities you will have available to you while improvising.

TRACK 8

Dominant Seventh Scales In All Twelve Keys

Track 9

Dominant Seventh Scales with Blue Notes

The blue notes (b3 and b5) can replace or be used in addition to the regular 3rd and 5th of the scale.

TRACK 10

Minor Pentatonic Scales In All Twelve Keys

These 5-note scales can replace or alternate with the regular seven-note scale for added color.

Major Pentatonic Scales In All Twelve Keys

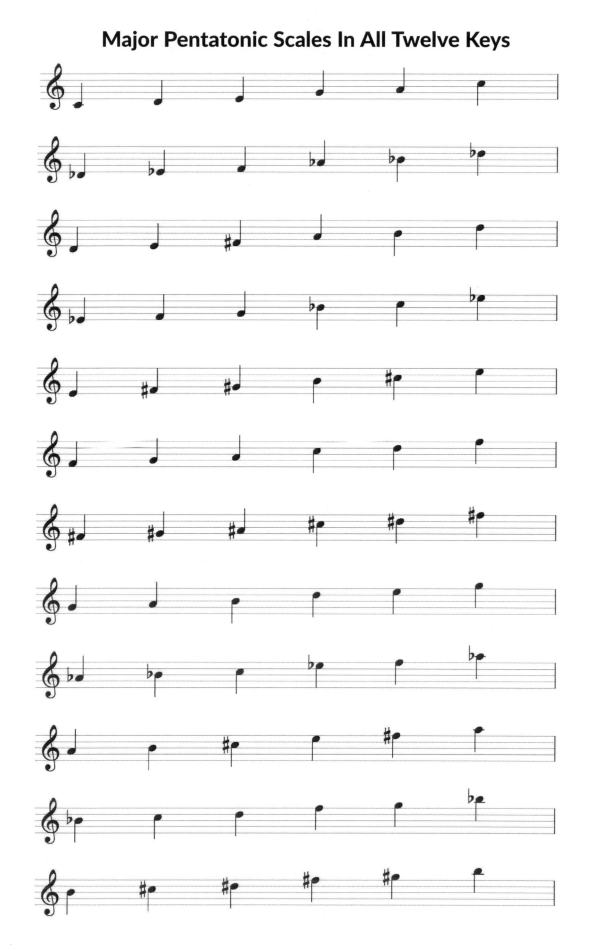

INTRODUCTIONS, BACKUP, AND ENDINGS

Introductions

The musical examples used in this section are based on the handiwork of some of the early blues fiddlers: Henry Sims, Bo Carter (also known as Bo Chatmon), Curtis Mosby, Leroy Pickett, Butch Cage, and Chasey Collins. Their styles are fairly representative of techniques used by the blues fiddlers as a whole.

There's an art to opening a tune, playing backup, and closing it. Developing skill in this area can help contribute to the successful presentation of the tune.

Although there are many ways to use the fiddle to start a blues tune, the most standard length introduction is four bars. To play any kind of introduction, previous knowledge of the key is essential. Quoting a theme from the melody is an obvious choice and always works in a pinch, but let's look at some other improvisational possibilities.

Leroy Pickett recorded six sides exclusively for Paramount between 1925 and 1927 with Viola Bartlette, Charles "Cow Cow" Davenport, Ma Rainey, and Ivy Smith. He opens his intro by starting on the 3rd of the key and then ends on the fifth. The tension created by the fifth is a nice lead into the melody.

TRACK 11

Henry Sims, also known as Son Sims, was born in 1900 and lived all of his life on the same plantation in Farrell, Mississippi. While in the army during World War I, Sims met Charlie Patton. They became very close friends and in 1929 recorded together for Paramount. In 1932, Muddy Waters and Scott Bowhandle joined Sims and formed a band, recording for the Library of Congress in 1942. Sims died in the 1960s in Farrell.

Here is an example of the kind of introduction Sims used. Like Pickett's introduction, it lands on the fifth of the key, lending a feeling of lack of resolution, which is an effective lead into the melody.

Bo Carter, whose real name was Armenter Chatmon, was born in 1893 in Bolton, Mississippi. His musical career started in 1917 when he joined a local string band. Soon after that he joined the family band, The Mississippi Sheiks.

Known mostly for his guitar playing and singing, Carter recorded on both fiddle and guitar with his brother Lonnie, as well as with musicians such as Texas Alexander, Alec Johnson, Charlie McCoy, Rosie Mae Moore, and Sonny Boy Nelson.

Carter toured extensively with the Mississippi Sheiks throughout the South, the Midwest, and the Northeast. In 1936 he lost his eyesight. When he died in Memphis in 1964, he was living in an unfurnished slum apartment. The occupants called him "Old Man" and his guitar was too worn with age and use to be played on again.

This opening line demonstrates an introduction with a more settled feeling because it closes on the tonic (the key).

Little is known about Curtis Mosby except that he recorded a few sides with Roosevelt Sykes and Mary Johnson in the early 1930s.

He's listed as a drummer and band leader, but I found him listed as a blues violinist on those sides.

To develop a solid working knowledge of the use of introductions in all keys, try composing an introduction and then transposing it into all twelve keys. The following example starts in the key of C and then moves up chromatically (in half steps) through the twelve keys. You can also try modulating this line or any line you create down in fifths (key of C, key of F, Bb, etc.) through all the keys or up in whole steps (key of C, key of D, E, F#, etc.) just to present yourself with an added challenge.

Sugarcane Harris and Dewey Terry
Photo courtesy of Jack Terry Music

Howard Armstrong
Photo courtesy of the American Legends Organization

 TRACK 12

Backup

When you play behind the lyrics, make sure you pay attention to how loud you play. The fiddle's sound tends to have a piercing nature, cutting through the air with more force than we often realize. If you can't hear the singer's lyrics, that's a good measurement to indicate that you are playing too loudly.

Chasey Collins played in the Chasey Collins Washboard Band, and was often referred to as "Dad." He was less accomplished technically, and often played on a one-string fiddle.

Collins seemed to prefer weaving simple lines behind the singer. While this line may not sound like a whole lot on its own, you'd understand how it adds flavor without competition if you could hear it behind a singer.

There are at least six different approaches to the fiddle's role when playing with a singer:

1) Silence except when soloing.

2) Mirror or echo the melody note for note.

3) Answer each vocal line with a complementary phrase.

4) Weave in and out; improvise freely behind the singer.

5) Use a walking ostinato or riff (a group of notes that you repeat with slight variations to frame the chords)

6) Use rhythmic double stops

Butch Cage was born to a sharecropper family on March 16, 1894, in Meadville, Mississippi. He was one of thirteen children, and his father died when he was ten. Uneducated, he got a job on a railroad in Baton Rouge. Later, Cage moved to Zachary, Louisiana, where he recorded with his partner, Willie Thomas. Cage gained popularity when he and Thomas appeared in 1960 at the Newport Folk Festival.

Butch Cage tended to use the third technique, answering each vocal line with a line on the fiddle.

TRACK 13

A walking ostinato or riff is simply a background line that is repeated throughout the twelve bar framework. Here's an example:

TRACK 14

Rhythmic double stops for backup developed as the violin became more actively used in R&B and jazz settings. Usually thought of as a solo instrument, the violin can be effectively used as a rhythm instrument too. A working knowledge of the chords is essential; learn them by practicing the 1 3 5 ♭7 of each key across the fingerboard.

The double stops can be sustained or rhythmized. If you use a dropping motion at the frog, you can get a very percussive sound. Try to vary inflections and swing a little so that the accompaniment isn't flat and unsupported.

For instance, if you're practicing double stops on a C7 chord, don't limit yourself by practicing from C to C. Identify the four chord tones (i.e. C E G B♭) and then play them all starting on your open G string and moving up to the Bb on your E string or even higher if you know how to shift.

You can combine two chord tones (root, third, fifth, or seventh) in any way you wish, to create a harmonic backdrop for another soloist, or to fit in with the rhythm section. I like to keep my double-stops on the G and D strings because the higher strings tend to compete with the soloist. Try adding your own rhythms to each double stop.

TRACK 15

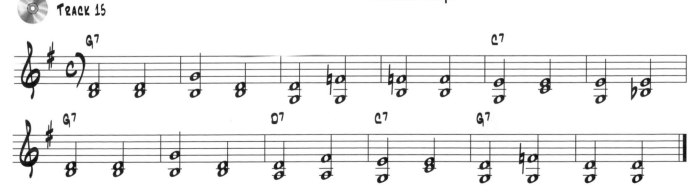

In this second example, the figures are rhythmized and sparse. The rhythmic motif helps spice things up, while keeping the violin out of the way of the soloist. Notice the dissonant, yet pleasing sound the seventh against the third or root can provide.

Here's a busier backdrop. All the notes chosen conform to the notes governed by each chord symbol, not the key signature. There are some syncopated rhythms introduced in the third and fifth measures, as well as some on-the-beat walking lines. Any one of these rhythmic figures could be used successfully throughout, or you can choose to vary your figures. Ask your fellow musicians what they prefer!

Armstrong family, 1925, Knox County, TN.
From the collection of Marshall Wyatt

Endings

Basically, you can either end in unison with the other musicians, or tag a short solo on at the end. The tag needn't be terribly different from the introduction, but should generally close on the tonic. Here are two examples of endings Bo Carter was particularly known for. In both cases, he started on the fifth of the key and ended on the tonic.

Track 16

For a more interesting twist, try closing on the seventh of the key:

Will Batts Novelty Band, 1939, Memphis, TN
From the collection of Marshall Wyatt

FIDDLING WITH FUNK

When I interviewed blues fiddler Papa John Creach in the early eighties, he told me a story about how he'd gone to hear Noel Pointer perform with his band. Pointer was famous for choosing really hot funky rhythm sections and superimposing improvised classical sounding lines over the top. Apparently Pointer was honored that Creach had come to hear him play, and when they were introduced afterwards, was probably hoping for some words of support. What he heard instead, was "Boy, you got to get down. You got to get nasty. You've got to make that violin scratch and moan."

When you think about it, we spend up to hundreds of hours in the beginning trying to get a smooth sound with the bow; we work on creamy changes of direction and resonant tone, as we're focussed on holding the bow properly. Naturally, when it comes time to play in a style such as the blues, the bow hand is already sailing on automatic, using the instructions it's already received.

To make the transition into a bluesy tone, you're going to have to be willing to give some of that up. This means accentuating some lines just at the frog (jazz violinist Stuff Smith was famous for playing at the frog to create his gruff horn-like sound); stopping the bow just short of the rhythmic value of your line's notes so that there's some space between notes; moving the bow rhythmically in relationship to the left hand's line; and varying the pressure of the bow on the string.

Rhythmically speaking, you will also need to learn how to play all of your basic rhythms laid back a little on the beat. Many players rush their notes, so it's well worth practicing entire solos just on one rhythm at a time (quarter notes, eighths, triplets, and sixteenths to start) without rushing. Again, this doesn't mean that the bow should necessarily be moving in a legato fashion. Start legato to get the rhythm lined up properly, and then try to put a subtle but crisp articulation on each note.

Converting to a funky, bluesy sound also means that instead of trying to make up new line after new line, you are going to need to learn how to create riffs (repeated musical phrases), use slide technique, weave pentatonic lines into your solos, and "squeeze the water" out of held notes by slight increases in bow pressure and speed as you hold the note.

Evenly tempered vibrato will not get you there! As we've already discussed, vibrato must be used as a seasoning, with variations in width and speed.

If we listen to the use of strings throughout history in blues and rock, most pop artists — dating all the way back to Buddy Holly and the Beatles — preferred to hire classical-sounding string players who read charts. Even in jazz, Charlie Parker's concept of recording with strings was to use drippingly classical arrangements with bebop saxophone! I can't tell you how many artists have sent me their CDs labeling themselves as funk-oriented violinists, and all I've heard was a funky band with a classical-sounding violin superimposed over the top (sweet vibrato, legato bow "glued" to the string). This doesn't mean they weren't playing great lines, but great lines don't equal gut-bucket, soul-wrenching, string-tearing, expressive blues fiddle.

To get started, try listening to artists like Papa John Creach, Sugarcane Harris, Randy Sabien, and Heather Hardy, to name a few, to develop a sense of other possibilities on the instrument.

Amplification

You have undoubtedly spent a good deal of time selecting the acoustic instrument and bow you prefer, the string brand, type of rosin, and if you're like me, have visited a luthier to monkey with your sound post setting—all in an effort to achieve the sound you prefer.

It's no different with amplification choices. Some artists prefer standing at a mic with their acoustic while others use a clip-on mic or electronics inside or attached to their bridge. I have not found just one solution for all situations. For situations requiring a genuinely solid boost, like playing with horns and drums, a solidi-body becomes essential to avoid feedback when you boost your volume.

At the Fourth American Jazz String Summit, September, 2000, each of the players and clinicians had a different solution for amplification. There was a five-string Zeta violin, an Aceto five-string violin, several Baggs systems, and so on. Since there were over 100 violinists in the hall that day, this event demonstrates the fact that no one system can satisfy the needs of each and every player. With each decade, more and more awesome makers have entered the field. Now we get to choose our sound as well as the look of our instrument from a wide array of possibilities.

Your local music store may only carry one or two out of the options available. Your best resource is **Electric Violin Shop**, the only store in the world that specializes in carrying everything.

While budget is certainly an important factor, you will also need to consider how much volume you'll need, the degree of tonal control you want, ergonomic factors, and the image you wish to convey.

Ergonomics

Make sure you try any solid-body you plan to purchase. It may look flashy in the picture, but could be too heavy, or have a built-in shoulder rest that isn't appropriate for your build.

Volume
Pickups

Pickups that attach to the bridge are excellent for a modest boost. Without a preamp, they will provide you with enough power to be heard in a small club with a small ensemble, but in most cases, give little ability to boost beyond that. The preamp is a small box that you can use as an intermediary between your pickup and amp or house system. It provides tonal control, as well as the capability to boost the volume. Some pickups can ruin your bridge because of how they attach, so factor that in when you choose a system.

Transducer Bridge

A transducer bridge generally boosts the outgoing signal significantly more than a pickup. It is a violin bridge that has the electronics built into it. It usually has a wire coming out of the bridge that attaches to a fixture with a guitar jack on the side of the violin. You plug one end of the cord into the fixture and the other into your preamp or amp.

Sometimes the use of a transducer bridge can alter the tone of your acoustic violin—for the better or for the worse, depending on the maker. Be prepared for a change, or use a second violin for the bridge.

Solid-Body

The solid-body violin has little or no sound when played acoustically. It has to be plugged into an amp to be heard. There is no danger of feedback when you boost the volume, and most solid-body violins will provide you with all the volume you need. You can also choose between fairly tame-looking instruments, to really flashy designs that distinguish you when you step onto stage.

Tone

Most systems provide a "one-size fits all" type of tone. No matter what your instrument sounds like acoustically, they will filter its sound through their tonal orientation. Each solid-body violin offers its own definition of sound as well. If you use NS Design as an example, they offer a number of different solid-body violins as does Mark Wood Violins and Yamaha. In addition to variations in appearance, the tone of each of these instruments is attenuated slightly differently. Make sure you buy something you will enjoy for a long time, but remember to use a preamp for ultimate control over your tone and volume.

Julie's Equipment

Bartlett Fiddle Mic

Eastman Series+ Violin with built-in technology (can be played acoustically or plugged in)

NS NXT Design Solid-Body Violin

SPUR amplified acoustic violin (designed to be played while plugged in)

Fishman Loudbox Amp (Mini BT 60-watt 1 x 6.5-inch Acoustic Combo Amp)

Fishman Loudbox Artist Amp (BT 120-watt 1x8" Acoustic Combo Amp with Tweeter & Bluetooth

L.R. Baggs Para DI acoustic Preamp

Tech 21 SansAmp Para Driver V2 DI Preamp

Zoom A1X Four Acoustic Instrument Multi-Effect Processor

Boss RC-300 Loop Station 3-track Looper Pedal

Electro-Harmonix Micro POG Polyphonic Octave Generator Pedal

BOSS ME-80 Guitar Multi-Effects Pedal

THE BLUES FIDDLE TRADITION

Few of today's violinists and fiddlers are aware of the black blues fiddlers of the late 1800s and early 1900s. These early pioneers of the fiddle stretched the instrument out of its traditional use in classical and fiddle literature, and forged a path of creativity by using the instrument to improvise. The left- and right-hand techniques they innovated on the instrument enabled them to mirror and interact with blues singers in a funky, earthy manner and their use of syncopation affected white fiddling throughout the South.

When the first African slaves were sold to the residents of Jamestown, Virginia, in 1619, the musical climate of the European settlers was relatively undeveloped. Their first priority was survival, and leisure time was limited. European folk and classical music were the only forms of music present. The fiddle, because it was easily transportable and made out of materials that were quickly accessible in America, was used as a spirited rhythmical force for square dances, and for entertainment at social gatherings. Native American music, while an integral force in the evolution of the music of Louisiana, had no influence throughout the rest of the South due to the separatist attitude of the settlers.

At first, slaves were not permitted any activity outside hard labor. They were denied education or access to materials for visual arts or drumming because slavers, knowing that communication between slaves would be heightened by such activities, feared rebellion. Singing was permitted, but the subject matter was restricted.

Frances Anne Kemble, an Englishwoman who lived on a Georgia plantation from 1838 to 1839, wrote in her diary:

I have heard that many of the masters and overseers on these plantations prohibit melancholy tunes or words, and encourage nothing but cheerful music and senseless words, deprecating the effect of sadder strains upon the slaves, whose peculiar musical sensibility might be expected to make them especially excitable by any songs of a plaintive character and have any reference to their particular hardships.

Frances Ann Kemble

As African slaves learned the English language and white European cultural customs, some plantation owners deemed these slaves "civilized" enough to serve in the big house, and musical opportunities for slaves opened up. During the second half of the seventeenth century, planters imported their favorite instruments from Europe and taught their slaves how to play them. These slaves were encouraged to develop their proficiency so that they might contribute to the pleasure and social prestige of their masters.

Ads appeared in papers such as the Virginia Gazette, the South Carolina Gazette, the Boston Evening Post, the Poughkeepsie Journal, and the South Carolina News offering high prices for Negro fiddlers. In 1690 there was a big scandal in Accomac County, Virginia, because the daughter of the Reverend Thomas Teakle got so carried away by a slave boy's fiddling that she and her friends danced all night.

> *RUN AWAY from the subscriber in Amelia, in the year 1766, a black Virginia born Negro fellow named Sambo, about 6 ft. High, about 32 years old. He makes fiddles, and can play upon the fiddle, and work at the carpenter's trade.*
>
> *Virginia Gazette*
> *August 18, 1768*

> *RUN AWAY - A Negro Man named Robert, 23 years old, about five feet, ten inches high; speaks good English, is a fiddler and took his fiddle with him. He also took with him a considerable quantity of clothing among which is a blue coat, snuff colored velvet breeches, velvet white jacket, etc. - had also considerable money.*
>
> *Godfred Wolner, Poughkeepsie Journal,*
> *November 24, 1791*

> *Whereas Cambridge, a Negro Man belonging to James Oliver of Boston doth absent himself sometimes from his Master: SAID NEGRO PLAYS WELL UPON A FLUTE AND NOT SO WELL ON A VIOLIN. This is to desire all Masters and Heads of Families not to suffer said Negro to come into Their Houses to teach their Prentices or Servants to play, nor on any other Accounts. All Masters of Vessels are also forbid to have anything to do with him on any Account, as they may answer it in the Law. N.B. Said Negro is to be sold: Enquire of said Oliver.*
>
> *Boston Evening Post*
> *October 24, 1743*

Some slaves became so accomplished on their instruments that they developed county and statewide reputations. Sy Gilliat, the body servant to Lord Botetourt, was the official fiddler for all of the Virginia state balls in the 1750s; it is said that he had a wardrobe of fifty suits! While music had been central to the black man's life in Africa, it had now become the key to survival in America. The rhythm of the work song provided fuel for many a weary laborer. Good singing work leaders commanded a premium price on the slave market. Most importantly, if a slave could excel instrumentally, he could avoid hard labor altogether and often live in relative luxury. Northup, a northern fiddler who was tricked into slavery in the early 1800s, wrote about his relationship to the fiddle:

> *Alas! Had it not been for my beloved violin, I scarcely can conceive how I could have endured the long years of bondage. It introduced me to great houses — relieved me of many days' labor in the field — supplied me with conveniences for my cabin — with pipes and tobacco, and extra pairs of shoes, and oftentimes led me away from the presence of a hard master, to witness scenes of jollity and mirth. It was my companion — the friend of my bosom — triumphing loudly when I was joyful, and uttering its soft, melodious consolations when I was sad. Often, at midnight, when sleep had fled affrighted from the cabin, and my soul was disturbed and troubled by the contemplation of my fate, it would sing me a song of peace.*
>
> *Solomon Northup*
> *1853, Twelve Years a Slave*

Many historians agree that New World blacks took to the fiddle because fiddle-type instruments existed in Africa. Instruments such as the bowed goge, the earthbow (a one-stringed instrument using a hole in the earth covered with animal hide as a resonator), or the Gonje (a one-stringed bowed instrument) could be considered members of the violin family. Evidence also exists that fifteenth-century European explorers used violins to barter with African tribes.

"———————————"

One day, I see Marse Thomas a twistin' de ears on a fiddle and rosinin' de bow. Then he pull dat bow 'cross de belly of dat fiddle. Something bust loose in me and sing all thru my head and tingle in my fingers. I made up my mind, right then and dere, to save and buy me a fiddle. I got one dat Christmas, bless God! I learn and been playin' de fiddle ever since. I pat one foot while I'm playin'. I kept on playin' and pattin' dat foot for thirty years. I lose dat foot in a smash-up wid a highway accident, but (when) I play de old tunes on dat fiddle at night, dat foot seem to be dere at de end of dat leg and pats just de same. Sometime I ketch myself lookin' down to see if it have come back and joined itself up to dat leg, from de very charm of de music I makin' wid de fiddle and de bow... Who I marry? I marry Ellen Watson, as pretty a ginger cake nigger as ever fried a batter cake and rolled her arms' up in a wash tub. How I git her? I never git her; dat fiddle get her... What church I belong to? None. Dat fiddle draws down from heaven all de sermons dat I understand. I sings de hymns in de way I praise and glorify de Lord.*

Andy Brice, Winnsboro, S.C.

*Eileen Southern, Readings in Black American Music (New York,; Norton, 1971); p. 118 - 119

One-stringed American fiddles were very common among blues fiddlers. Chasey Collins, One-String Sam, and many others quite capably teased the sound out of such instruments. Big Bill Broonzy describes his early instrument-making experiences as testimony: "When I was about ten years old I made a fiddle out of a cigar box, guitars out of goods boxes for my buddy Louis Carter, and we would play for the white people's picnics...my fiddle didn't haven't but one string on it."

Slave fiddlers played square dance tunes, old-time tunes, and classical music for their masters. For their own people the music often took on a different sound, becoming a synthesis of African strains and white influences, fueled by explosive pent-up emotion.

Although the fiddle was not the only instrument played by slaves, the only other one that approached it in popularity was another instrument with African relatives, the banjar or banjo. The popularity of the violin and the banjo was encouraged by the accessibility of construction materials in America.

Christians considered the fiddle a devil's instrument, and as Christianity entered the slave community, the fiddle did not share a position in the development of gospel music. It reentered the picture only with the advent of minstrels. Although the early black minstrels were more prone to use the banjo, tambourine, and bones during their performances, the first man to popularize the minstrel shows was a fiddler named Daniel Decatur Emmett. In 1834 he and his group, The Virginia Minstrels, were the first of a chain of about seventy-five companies to put on black-face minstrel shows.

It's difficult to identify how the fiddle was being used during the end of the 1800s. Ironically, the best proof of its activities can be found in police records from raids: it was common to find a band with several fiddles, clarinet, banjo, and percussion that had been arrested in a back-room bar. The next documented era of black fiddling doesn't surface until the 1900s with the commercialization of the blues.

Keep in mind that when the first blues fiddlers were recorded, they were earning their living played a wide spectrum of minstrel show music, country dances, ragtime, vaudeville, and jazz. Many players belonged to string-bands and performed at picnics, dances, weddings, and parties.

Big Bill Broonzy, in his autobiography, says of the black blues fiddlers, "They didn't call what they played blues...They called it Negro reels." It is important to remember that the blues was sung and played long before it became popular on the commercial market.

The first twelve-bar blues to be published was written by a white violinist named Hart Wand, a dance-band leader in Oklahoma. Hart avidly listened to black music and played a blues-like melody during his daily practice time. One day, after hearing the tune, a black porter from Dallas said, "That gives me the blues to go back to Dallas."

Hart named the tune "The Dallas Blues" and published it in March 1912, shortly before Arthur Seal published "Baby Seal Blues" (August 1912) and W. C. Handy published "The Memphis Blues" (September 1912). These three tunes became extremely popular, and entertainers everywhere began incorporating blues material into their acts. Hundreds of songs were composed in the style of "The Dallas Blues" and "The Memphis Blues."

Black instrumentalists benefited from the popularity of the blues, and could now get work in orchestras and dance bands or make money playing in smaller groups. Fiddler Lonnie Chatmon, known for his comment "Work ain't good to eat!," was one of many musicians who

happily gave up labor in the fields for a life on the road as an entertainer.

Prior to the popularity of the blues, record companies would not record black musicians. Perry Bradford, recording director for Okeh records, was the fist to manufacture what were known as "Race Records." Paramount and Victor, seeing that these records were selling phenomenally well in black communities, followed Okeh's example.

At first, these recordings were made in the record studios. But many musicians lived in backwoods country. They were hard to find, and they were inexperienced in the ways of the commercial world. They often felt intimidated by the stark, unmusical feeling of the studios.

To loosen up the sessions, many of the musicians were given liquor as a part of their payment, and heavy drinking was common at recording sessions.

With Victor in the lead, the companies began doing extensive field recordings, sending representatives into different counties to scout out new talent through hearsay and auditions. A date would be set, and the company would arrive with its equipment and set up in a storefront or any available space. Lonnie Johnson was discovered in just this manner. He won a talent scout contest at the Booker Washington Theater eighteen weeks in a row and got an eleven-year recording contract with Okeh.

The popularity of a record determined whether the musician or group recorded again. It was standard for these groups to include fiddle, but none of the fiddlers got top billing at that time, as many do nowadays.

The fiddler would improvise behind the singer unless he had a favorite line that he liked to repeat. The number of solos played differed from recording to recording, depending on his capabilities as a player and the preference of the group leader.

Thanks to the opportunism and competitiveness of the music industry, the music of the black blues fiddlers was sought out and preserved. As the reels turned, history was recorded.

" ━━━━━━━━━━━━━━ **"**

Blues works in many ways, happy and sad. It can do a lot of strange things to the human mind. I've seen the form of blues that can cause death. If you play those blues all night at a dance where there's a lot of booze in the house, you'll have fights.*

Clarence Gatemouth Brown

Blues fiddle died out in the late twenties. Some historians say, like all musical trends, that it had outlived itself. I was never satisfied with that explanation. While working on my National Public Radio Series, **The Talking Violin,** I had the opportunity to interview jazz bassist Milt Hinton. He gave me another possible explanation:

" ━━━━━━━━━━━━━━ **"**

Chicago had all these great violin players, black violin players. Every theater had an orchestra play the music for the screen, because there was no sound. We had a neighborhood theater with a violin, a drum, and a piano. It was in 1929 when Al Jolson made the first sound movie, "The Jazz Singer." That's when the whole conversion came; every theater got rid of all of its musicians.

But the violin players had no place to go. There were loads of black clubs in Chicago for black musicians to work in, but they didn't use violins. There was booze being drunk, and people were dancing. So there was no room for violins. So this was the end, 1930, '31, '32, '33 was the end of the black violin players. And they began to fade.

All of these wonderful violin players — I don't see them. They disappeared. But one afternoon I was delivering papers. I'd go around to peoples' homes and collect for my paper, the Chicago Herald Examiner, and I'd usually go to the back door. There I found them. A great deal of these violin players were from New Orleans. And now since they don't have any jobs playin' violin, they were cigar makers. And on their screened-in back porches, they were rolling cigars, making cigars, and taking them downtown to sell them to the wealthy people in the downtown department stores. This is how they survived when they didn't have work.

Milt Hinton

*Robert Neff and Anthony Connor, Blues (Boston; Godine; 1975) p. 58

HOW TO READ THE TRANSCRIPTIONS

During the days of slavery, black fiddlers could learn white European classical technique or folk fiddling, or both, depending on their location and slave-owner. In describing specific sounds, classical terminology has been used below:

Right Hand:

Downbow

The bow is pulled from frog to tip.

Upbow

The bow is pushed from tip to frog.

Slur

The notes indicated by the slur mark are all played within one upbow or one downbow.

The Bounced Bow or Spiccato

The bow is bounced on the string.

The Stopped Bow/Detache Lance

The notes are played with a distinct separation between each, almost stopping the movement of the bow briefly between each note.

The Blues Shimmer or Tremolo

This sound is created by moving the bow very quickly up and down on the string at the tip of the bow. I've shown two methods to indicate the use of tremolo: "Trem" and slashes across the stem of the note. The dashes to the right of "Trem" indicate the duration of the bowing.

Tremolo is evenly paced, whereas the blues shimmer is much faster and uses less bow.

Plucked Notes or Pizzicato

Secure your right thumb under the upper right corner of the fingerboard and pluck the strings with your index finger over the edge of the fingerboard.

Inflections

Accentuate the notes indicated by increasing the bow's pressure.

Left Hand

Standard notation has been used to indicate the fingerings: first finger - 1; second finger - 2; third finger - 3; and pinky - 4.

Slides

There are many types of slides that can be created. See page 10 for details. Slides are indicated by a line coming up into the note, down out of it, or both.

Trills

Rapidly alternate between the two notes for the time limit indicated.

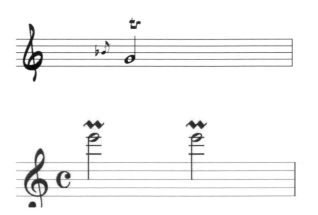

Vibrato

A wide, hysterical vibrato is used when indicated by this symbol.

The Mobile Strugglers with Charles Jones and James Fields on violin. 1949.
From the collection of Marshall Wyatt

THE TUNES

The solos in the next section demonstrate each player's individual style in the blues. Due to publishing restraints, I've written tunes "in the style of" each player. Biographical information varies depending on the popularity of the fiddler during his lifetime. Each solo in this book has been written in the style of the player. I have also made sure that most of the twelve keys are represented within the tunes.

It is actually pretty hard to be accurate about keys when listening to old 78s, and it's doubtful that every band even tuned to what we call concert pitch (A = 440) today. While I tried to stay as close to the style of the player as possible, I also designed the tunes to assist you in learning about options for blues phrasing, and the practice tracks are there to help you develop your improvisational skills in the style.

Listen to the tunes on the practice CD first and pick out ones you really like. Alternate between learning it by ear to strengthen your listening skills, and by reading the solo — which, in turn, will strengthen your reading skills.

When you solo over the backing tracks available on iTunes, try to keep your lines simple at first, and stay focussed on where you are within the form and the notes available to you per chord change. More sophisticated lines and speed will develop naturally out of tasty, well-placed lines that are grounded in knowing what chord is being played.

Think of the country blues as containing three "quadrants:" the first quadrant has one chord lasting four bars; the second quadrant has two chords distributed evenly: the fourth of the key moving back home to the tonic; and the third quadrant contains more harmonic motion as it moves through the fifth of the key, the fourth, and then back home.

It is essential that you seek out and jam with as many other musicians as you can. If for some reason this simply isn't possible, jam with CDs or blues tracks on Youtube. You can use artist's blues CDs or a "music minus one" accompaniment from Jamey Aebersold's company, Jazz Aides, like "Nothing But The Blues" or "Blues in All Twelve Keys."

Julie with Claude "Fiddler" Williams and his first wife, Mabel, in Kansas City, just before Claude performed with Wynton Marselis.

THE BLUES FIDDLERS

Clifford Hayes

A fiddler as well as a band leader, Hayes recorded in 1924 and 1927. He is known for his work with Sara Martin's Jug Band, Clifford's Louisville Jug Band, the Old Southern Jug Band, the Dixieland Jug Blowers, and the Louisville Stompers. His use of octaves demonstrates a solid technical skill.

TRACK 17

BLUE MISS

BY JULIE LYONN LIEBERMAN

Lonnie Johnson

Lonnie Johnson was born Alonzo Johnson in New Orleans on Rampart and Franklin, February 8, during the 1880s. He had eleven musical sisters and one brother. Between 1914 and 1917, Lonnie played violin in his father's band in Storyville brothels and clubs. Then he went to England to entertain the troops. While he was away, an influenza epidemic tragically claimed most of his family. Upon his return, he bought a guitar and turned to music full time.

Lonnie had a long and productive career spanning forty years. He played violin, guitar, bass, mandolin, and banjo, and he sang. He was mainly known as a singer and guitarist, and few people knew that he was a violinist. This is understandable because he only recorded on violin early in his career.

At first, Lonnie played violin in the Charlie Creath Band. Then he formed a trio with DeLoise Searcy on piano and his brother James ("Steady Roll") on guitar and violin. No one is quite sure which brother played violin on the recordings made in Lonnie's name, but in an interview with Paul Oliver, Lonnie said that "Steady Roll" was the better violinist.

In 1965, Lonnie retired and moved to Canada. He died in Toronto on June 16, 1970, after a serious car accident.

TRACK 18

TEARS ARE FALLING

BY JULIE LYONN LIEBERMAN

Eddie Anthony (Macon Ed)

Eddie Anthony was from Georgia. The only picture of him I've ever seen, portrays him as a left-handed fiddler. Anthony played in a string band with Peg Leg Howell and Henry Williams (Waymon "Sloppy" Henry) in Atlanta in the 1920s.

Anthony recorded with Peg Leg in 1927 and 1928 and with Williams in 1928. Using the pseudonym Macon Ed, he joined Tampa Joe to produce four sides in 1929 and 1930.

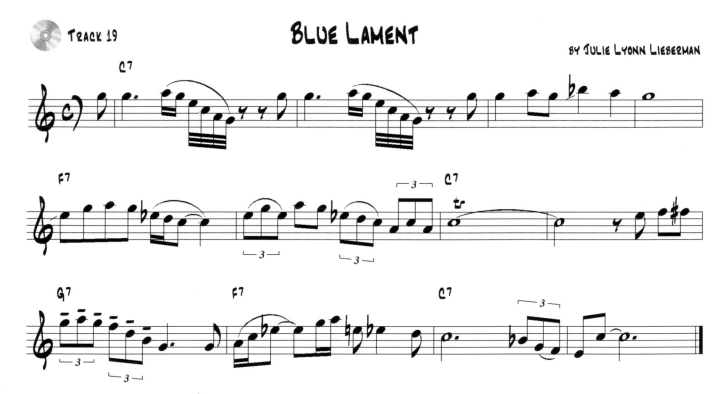

BLUE LAMENT

BY JULIE LYONN LIEBERMAN

TRACK 19

Tom "Bluecoat" Nelson

Tom Nelson recorded with T.C. Johnson in Memphis in 1929. Notice the staccato phrases and chromatic passing tones (b3 to 3) he incorporated into his playing style.

Track 20

J.J.'s Blues

BY JULIE LYONN LIEBERMAN

Nap Hayes

Little is know about Nap Hayes except that he recorded a few sides as both a singer and fiddler with T.C. Johnson and Matthew Prater in 1928.

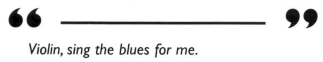

Violin, sing the blues for me.

T.C. Johnson

Milton Robie

Robie was in one of the early Memphis jug bands. Blues historian Paul Oliver describes their jug band style of blues as "blues of a slightly hokum kind very often with cheerful ribbin, veiled ribaldry and sometimes…a melancholy beautifully resolved completeness."

BLUES BE KIND

BY JULIE LYONN LIEBERMAN

©1985 Huiksi Music

Lonnie Chatmon

The Chatmon family came from Mississippi. As slaves, Ezell and Ferdinand Chatmon learned music from their father. Either Ezell or one of his descendants, Henderson, married another slave musician and after emancipation had eleven sons and one daughter. In an interview with Paul Oliver, Bo Chatmon recalled the names of eight of his ten siblings: Lonnie, Edgar, Willie, Lamar, Sam, Harry, Charlie, and Laurie.

All of the Chatmon children learned how to play instruments at an early age. Bo, Lonnie, Sam, and Harry were particularly adept at playing a number of instruments well. Individually and collectively, the Chatmons (including their half brother Walter Vincson) recorded well over 150 sides, 104 of which included either Lonnie or Bo on fiddle.

The Chatmon's recording career began in 1929 when Lonnie, Bo, Sam, and Walter were playing at a white square dance in Itta Bena. A local record dealer named Ralph Lembo heard them and arranged their first recording with Okeh Records in Shreveport, Louisiana. This was followed by work for Bluebird, Columbia,

Brunswick, Vocalion, Melotone, Champion, Paramount, and Varsity. On some of these labels they played backup for musicians like Texas Alexander and Charlie McCoy.

As performers, the Chatmons were mainly known as the Mississippi Sheiks. Depending on which combination of brothers were recording on what label, they used the pseudonyms, The Mississippi BlackSnakes, the Mississippi Hot Footers, the Mississippi MudSteppers, the Carter Brothers, the Chatmon Brothers, the Jackson Blues Boys, and the Down South Boys.

Lonnie, born in Bolton, Mississippi in the early 1890s, learned how to fiddle from his father.

He hated farming and devoted most of his time to music. "Work ain't good to eat." He reputedly said.

Rumor has it that Lonnie's brothers stopped playing with him because he always wanted the spotlight and usually tried to make off with the largest share of money, which he would then spend on alcohol, gambling, and women.

In 1937, Lonnie moved to Anguilla; later he returned to Bolton, where he worked at various jobs until his death in 1942 or 1943.

Lonnie had good technique: he could play in position, had superior bowing ability, played in tune, and had a nice rolling vibrato.

TRACK 23

SAD-EYED BLUES

BY JULIE LYONN LIEBERMAN

James Cole

Cole, a guitarist and fiddler, sometimes known as "Big Boy Ben," accompanied Tommie Bradley, Buster Johnson, Walter Cole, and Jack O'Diamonds.

GRAVEDIGGER BLUES

BY JULIE LYONN LIEBERMAN

TRACK 24

Will Batts

Will Batts was considered one of the best blues fiddlers in the Memphis area. He played with Jack Kelly, Dan Sane, Frank Stokes, and D.M Higgs in the 1920s and 30s in a group called the South Memphis Jug Band. One of the longest surviving jug bands, they were originally called Jack Kellys' Jug Busters, but ARC Records changed their name for recording purposes. One of their steady gigs was in the Peabody Hotel in Memphis, where a pianist or musical saw player would join them.

Batt recorded thirteen sides with the South Memphis Jug Band between 1929 and 1933. In 1939 he recorded again using the pseudonym Bast. This session with Jack Kelly, Dan Sing (Sane) and D.M. Higgs, produced ten sides.

Track 25

MOVING RIGHT ALONG BLUES

BY JULIE LYONN LIEBERMAN

Charlie Pierce

In the 1920s, many jug bands began making their appearance in the South. Most of them were made up of kazoos, washboards, tin cans, empty bottles, washtubs, guitars, fiddles, and other assorted instruments. These jug bands performed uptempo blues.

Charlie Pierce played in the Memphis Jug Band. Though his tone was often raspy, he played with tremendous gusto!

TRACK 26

GRITS AND GRAVY BLUES

BY JULIE LYONN LIEBERMAN

Carl Martin

Carl Martin was born in 1906 in Big Stone Gap, Virginia, and was raised in Knoxville. His father was a stonemason, violinist, and guitarist. His older brother, Roland, also a musician, taught Martin how to play the violin, guitar, mandolin, and string bass.

Martin joined Howard Armstrong and Ted Bogan in 1932. They toured together and settled in Chicago, where they began performing again in 1966 after dropping out of sight for a

number of years. During the interim, Martin did some work with Amos Easton and Big Bill Broonzy.

Martin's solos are unique because he is one of the few recorded blues fiddlers who plucked rather than bowed some of his solos. His fiddle technique was probably influenced by his mandolin work.

©1985 Huiksi Music

Remo Biondi

A guitarist, arranger, and violinist, Remo Biondi recorded for United and Vocalion, did a considerable amount of pop studio work, and became concertmaster of Gene Krupa's band in the early 1940s. He is in two 16mm films: one with Krupa (1942) and another (on guitar) with Joe Marsala (1945).

According to blues collector Bob Koester, who now owns the United sides as well as the two films, Biondi was a shy, retiring man with an Italian mustache and a tiny amp that he kept turned down so low you had to sit next to him to hear him play.

When Roosevelt Sykes recorded for United in 1952, Biondi worked for no pay because his union status prohibited him from taking other work such as club jobs and recording sessions. He was a radio staff musician at the time.

Biondi's playing demonstrates technique, creativity, and an electric violin sound that helped set the standard for future players.

TRACK 28

HOTTER THAN BLUES

BY JULIE LYONN LIEBERMAN

Don "Sugarcane" Harris

Don Harris, who received his nickname "Sugarcane" from Johnny Otis because he was quite the ladies' man, started his life on June 18, 1938 in Pasadena, California. The son of carnival performers, he studied classical violin with L.C. Robinson from 1944 to 1954. He performed in local bars for a couple of years following high school until he met Dewey Terry. They formed the Don and Dewey Duo, toured the West coast as a part of the Johnny Otis show, and recorded for Specialty and Rush records. The sides "Soul Motion" and" Stretchin' Out" demonstrate particularly hot violin solos.

After his days with Dewey, Sugarcane worked with Little Richard, Frank Zappa (Hot Rats) and John Mayall, and started his solo career in 1970. Though he also played guitar, harmonica, and piano, he was mostly known for his hot blues-rock electric violin. As you will notice in this sample of his style, he could weave his solo around little more than four or five notes, and create an incredible solo. Most of his compositions are built on simple two and three-chord progressions, and it is fairly typical of his solos to focus on riffs and textures over melodic lines.

Don Sugarcane Harris
Photo courtesy of Jack Terry Music and Randy Resnick

TRACK 29

STRETCH IT

BY JULIE LYONN LIEBERMAN

Howard Armstrong

Born in Lafayette, Tennessee, in the early 1900s, Howard Armstrong learned how to play the fiddle at a very early age, but his mother and sister would only let him play hymns and spirituals. In his early teens he learned some fiddle tunes from Roland Martin (Carl Martin's brother) and at age sixteen went on the road.

In the 1930s, Armstrong recorded with Roland and Carl Martin in a group called The Tennessee Chocolate Drops and a year later formed the Four Keys String Band which included Ted Bogan and Carl Martin. They started in Huntington, West Virginia, and played through-out the South at square dances, picnics, churches, and wherever else they could get work.

Armstrong recorded in 1934 with Ted Bogan, using the pseudonym "Louie Bluie". In the 1960s he reappeared in the group Martin, Bogan, and Armstrong, performing at folk festivals throughout the country.

Self-educated, Howard Armstrong learned seven languages. His colorful imagination and love for music are evident in his playing. Here's a story Howard told me about his first violin:

66 ——————— 99

But one day, I told my daddy, 'I got to have a violin.' He said, 'Well, you know, I - I got nine kids. There's eleven of us in the family. My salary (we didn't say salary) my pay isn't enough to buy you a fiddle. But I tell you what I'll do, son: You go around the trash piles, in the alleys, and see if you can find an old seasoned dirt box.' And I did. And the old man came home in the evenin', from work — he worked til five o'clock at the blast furnace — and he took out a pocket knife and cut me out a violin. I wish to this day that I had it! And he carved the neck out and everything; then he varnished it with some — back then they had a kind of varnish you had in a can. Looked like it was a cross between lacquer and varnish — it dried real fast. They called it japalac. And it had the color right into the liquid. It wasn't just clear varnish like shellac or anything.

And he japalacqed that fiddle for me. And he cut out everything for it, but the strings. He cut the bridge out of a piece of hard wood, and round the fringe of the woods where we lived they had dogwood: hard wood trees with those pretty blossoms on it. And a dead dogwood tree is hard as ivory, almost. I got him a chunk of that dogwood and made me a tailpiece, and cut the pegs out, and a stick to bow it.

I - I - I was thrilled to no end! And I almost never, never, never got home, stopping beside the road, playing for the chipmunks, squirrels, or what — birds — I scared everything, I guess!

Howard Armstrong

Blues on the Riviera

Track 30

By Julie Lyonn Lieberman

©1985 Huiksi Music

Courtesy of the Howard Armstrong Collection

Papa John Creach

Many of Papa John Creach's fans do not realize that he spent over thirty-five years playing blues and jazz prior to his debut as a rock violinist with the Jefferson Starship in 1970, and that when Creach started out on the violin back in the late twenties, his first training was in classical music.

One of ten children, Creach was born in Beaver Falls, Pennsylvania on May 28, 1917. When he was about ten years old, his uncle taught him how to play the violin and he continued his studies with a local violin teacher after he and his family moved to Chicago several years later. Gradually, Creach began to jam with local jazz musicians. He learned about chord changes and how to read charts, and began to gig in local clubs.

In interview, Creach remembered his audience's attitude towards the violin in those early days with a twinkle in his eye: "Black people always thought that the violin was a starvation box. They would call it a sissy instrument, so it was unusual for them to see me stand up in a black club and play the blues and jazz. I was a freak! I used to fool them all the time. I would come into a club and put my violin out of view on stage. I'd go up to the bar and get me a little sip. Then I would open up my case and rosin up my bow and lay it on the piano. I'd take out my violin and they would say, 'Oh, no, Jack Benny!' I wouldn't pay no attention to them. I'd just gear up my amplifier real loud and pick up my violin and I'd shower it out WHOOM! Then they'd say 'ooo, you sure can play that thing.' I never had no trouble in that club after that."

Along with jazz violinist Stuff Smith, who began playing amplified violin in 1936, Creach was one of the earliest electric violinists. His first electric violin was a National with a built-in volume control which he began using in 1943.

After countless jazz and R&B gigs throughout the United States and Canada with his own groups: The Chocolate Music Bars and The Johnny Creach Trio as well as on board a luxury liner with The Shipmates, Creach's fortunate moment came when, while gazing at the local musician's union bulletin board, he met drummer Joey Covington, who subsequently introduced him to the Jefferson Airplane. Over the next four years, Creach worked concurrently with the Jefferson Starship, Hot Tuna, and his own band until he finally turned his energies in full to his own band.

During this period of time, while working on a big project, someone referred to him as "Father John." He did not like that name and while discussing it with Joey Covington, they came up with "Papa John" from calling their fathers papa. The nickname not only stuck, but became a very catchy commercial addition to his image.

When Papa John played, he modeled his approach to the violin after some of the great horn players — Ben Webster, Chu Berry, Coleman Hawkins, and Louis Armstrong — to name a few. "I play more like a horn, and try to acquire a nice fat round tone that's big; I usually play non-pressure on the violin." He advised his students to learn chord changes by running them like arpeggios. "Train the ears to hear the chords, and then you can start creating, or improvising." He also advised players to control their vibrato with selectivity, and to develop style, feeling, tone, intonation, harmony, theory, expression, and soul. "You have to concentrate in with your mind to do all that. See, some people say 'oh, it's the violin.' It's not the violin; the violin is just the instrument. It's the individual: you have to get it out there."

When I interviewed Papa John Creach in 1988, he talked about the blues with the intensity of experience:

66 _____ **99**

The blues is always based on somebody's misery — poor, hungry — back in that kind of moaning, groaning. It's always been very soulful. You don't have a lot of [harmonic] changes in the blues. It's not like jazz. So you have to express your thoughts, style, and music. You've got to moan. You've got to take your time; that's exactly what you've got to do to play the blues.

There are many things that come across my mind when I'm playing the violin. First the audience; next is the music; and then to try to put over the song; then, of course, you've got a group to think about. So you have to watch the people accompanying you; you have to take that into consideration. If I want to take a song and make it great, I will start creating it and build it up to a climax; but each time I play a chorus, I make it different; I keep changing it."

TRACK 31

PAPA'S BLUES

BY JULIE LYONN LIEBERMAN

Clarence Gatemouth Brown

Clarence Gatemouth Brown is recognized equally as a vocalist, guitarist and violinist. He also plays mandolin and harmonica and is known for his breakneck tempos. His music spans many styles including classical blues (leaning towards the style of his mentor, T-Bone Walker), swing, big band and Cajun. "I was once asked by T-Bone Walker, 'Gate, I wanna know one thing. Why do you try to play so many styles of music?' I said, 'Because in the first place, variety is the spice of life, T-Bone.'

Brown was born on April 18, 1924, in Vinton, Louisiana. He grew up in Orange, Texas, where he learned guitar and violin from his father Clarence Brown, Sr. He was nicknamed "Gatemouth" by a teacher because he had a such a loud voice. He began his professional life as a drummer in the early forties touring with Brown Skin Models. After a brief stint in the Engineer Corp. of the U.S. Army in 1946,

he continued touring with numerous orchestras and bands, including Big Mama Thornton, the artist upon which Janis Joplin based her style.

Gatemouth gradually broke away from being a sideman in the fifties, and established himself under his own name by developing two bands: one was a twenty-three piece black orchestra, and the other, all white, was a smaller group. This ingenious approach to racism enabled him to perform anywhere, including some of the classier white establishments of the fifties.

I met Gatemouth while hosting the Philadelphia Folk Festival fiddle workshop in 1976. I remember being impressed by how his lady friend gave him a shoulder massage to loosen him up before he performed. All of the other fiddlers on the workshop (of equal stature) looked like the land of the living dead in their neck and shoulder regions, and there he was, just as limber and relaxed as could be!

Clarence Gatemouth Brown
Photo courtesy of Susan Ruel

TRACK 32

Blues At Dawn

BY JULIE LYONN LIEBERMAN

Claude "Fiddler" Williams

Claude "Fiddler" Williams was born in Muskogee, OK, on February 22, 1908. He developed his fat, horn-like sound alongside Kansas City players such as Charlie Parker, Lester Young, Mary Lou Williams and members of the Oklahoma Blue Devils.

In his early days he worked with bands like The Pettifords Band, Andy Kirk's Twelve Clouds of Joy, Nat Cole's trio and the Basie Band. Claude preceded Freddie Green as Basie's first record-ed guitarist in 1936, and today is the last sur-vivor of the original band. Here's how he described his start on the violin to me back in the late eighties:

Photo by Russ Dantzler

66 ———————— **99**

I tell everybody about my brother-in-law. He's the one that started me out in everything. He knew quite a bit about strings. And he — he'd be sitting around the house playing the blues on an old guitar and he'd get tired and lay down, I'd pick up the guitar and almost play the same thing. When he saw I was interested, he went and bought a mandolin. And he would play the melody on the mandolin and show me the chords on the guitar. And we'd mess around for a while, and he'd lay the mandolin down, I'd pick the mandolin up and pick out some of the same things he was doing. And from the mandolin, we went and bought a cello. A cello isn't usually the right type of instrument for a string band, so they put bass strings on the cello for me to play bass. And we'd go round to different barber shops and hotels and be playing, and somebody would have to carry my cello for me. I was too small to carry it.

And finally, he traded the cello for a violin. I heard him tell my mother he's gonna get me something that never would go out of style. So, he took the cello down and traded it for a violin. And then he brought it home that day, about 5 or 6 o'clock.

Well, I knew how to play the fingering on it; all I had to get was the bowing part. I think the first number I played was "Got to See Your Mama Every Night or You Can't See Your Mama At All!"

Claude's life has been one long delicious cele-bration of music, particularly since age 70. He's been featured on CBS Sunday Morning News, and has played both Carnegie Hall and Lincoln Center several times. He even performed for Clinton's first inaugural. A happy outcome since his early days playing bass on cello!

Claude's 90th birthday was a normal one — he played five shows in five days in four cities! On his actual birthday, he played in a "Strung Together" concert in Northampton, MA, with five other fiddlers spanning 74 years in age. The wonderful CDs he's recorded in the last few decades give us a taste of his imagination, creativity, and the fire he imparts through his bow. His Kansas City roots provide him with a balance between bebop, blues, and a shape to his lines that distinguish him from any other player. But no matter how great he is on CD, his live performances are even better. Claude's passion for music comes to the forefront when he's sharing his music with live audiences!

TRACK 33

WHOSE BLUES

BY JULIE LYONN LIEBERMAN

Blues Fiddle Today

Even though Claude Williams is thought of as a jazz violinist, it was his playing that inspired this book. In 1976, after hosting the fiddle workshop at Philadelphia Folk Festival, a photographer from the festival called me and asked if I wanted to see the pictures he'd taken of me. When I arrived at his address in New York City, I discovered that it was the address of Music Sales Corporation. I thought he was the photographer for this publishing company, but learned while viewing his slides, that he was the (then) President! (Oops!) He introduced me to then editor Jason Shulman, who told me that my idea for writing a jazz violin book would never sell, but that if I wanted to write a blues fiddle book, he would publish it. He told me to buy the 1972 Sackville Recording of Jay McShann to listen to the fiddler on the album. I'd never heard of blues fiddle, nor had I heard of Claude Williams, but it was his playing on a tune called *Hootie Blues* that gave me the fever for the blues, and made me fall in love with Claude's style.

We don't have a group of violinists who specialize in blues fiddle today. Like the early blues fiddlers who could also play fiddle tunes and, in some cases, classical music, there are very few players who are mostly blues-oriented. Most contemporary players know and perform in a number of styles, including the blues. There are a few players, like Randy Sabien and Heather Hardy, who play a mean blues fiddle, though. Some artists have been described as being "blues based" in their sound. That means that they are emotional players, and are probably weaving the flatted third and fifth of the scale into their solos. Many bluegrass fiddlers (since bluegrass evolved from aspects of the blues) also flat those tones and use slide technique.

When you listen to a violinist sitting in with a blues or rock band, you can tell if they come from a blues lineage or a classical lineage. If they seem a little stiff, and their bow work is flashy and extremely precise bordering on staccato, they didn't come from the blues. Blues will turn both hands into mercurial messengers; borders will be hazed rather than clipped, and solos will be filled with syncopation, space (versus nonstop playing), muted transitions, and worlds of feeling.

Julie Lyonn Lieberman

DISCOGRAPHY

Compilation

Violin, Sing the Blues For Me (Old Hat Enterprises)

Armstrong, Howard

Barnyard Dance (Rounder Records 2003)

Martin, Bogan, and Armstrong (Folk Lyric 003)

Louie Bluie (Arhoolie 470)

Batts, Will

Low Down Memphis Barrelhouse Blues (Mamlish S-3803)

Brown, Clarence Gatemouth

House of Blues (Black Swan 80603)

The Blues Ain't Nothin' (Bluebird 33033)

Blackjack (First American Records IS-9002)

Brown, Jimmy

I Can See My Baby in My Dreams (Storyville SLP 180)

Cage, Butch

The Country Blues (Storyville 21014 SLP 129)

The Folk Music of the Newport Folk Festival 1959 - 1960 (Folkways FA-2431)

Country Negro Jam Session (Arhoolie 2018)

Chatmon, Lonnie

Stop and Listen: The Mississippi Sheiks (Mamlish, S3804)

Clay, Beauford

Blues in Trouble: Volume II (Arhoolie F1012)

Collins, Chasey

Jug, Jook, & Washboard Bands (Arhoolie BC2)

Creach, Papa John

Papa Blues (Bee Bump Records)

Hardy, Heather

I Believe

Violins

Harris, Don Sugarcane

USA Union (Polydor)

Pierce, Charlie

Jug, Jook, and Washboard Bands (Arhoolie BC2)

Sabien, Randy

Fiddlehead Blues (Fiddlehead Music)

Sims, Henry Son

Mississippi Blues 1927 - 1941 (Belzona L1001)

Williams, Claude "Fiddler"

Live at J's (Smithsonian Folkways)

Swingtime in New York (Progressive Records)

BIBLIOGRAPHY

The Man From Muskogee (Sackville 3005)

Botkin, B.A., *Lay My Burden Down*, Chicago: University of Chicago Press, 1945.

Charters, Samuel, *The Country Blues*, New York: Da Capo, 1975.

Charters, Samuel, *The Country Blues*, New York: De Capo, 1959.

Charters, Samuel, *The Bluesmen*, New York: Oak, 1967.

Chase, Gilbert, *America's Music*, New York: McGraw Hill, 1955.

Cook, Bruce, *Listen to the Blues*, New York: Scribner's, 1973.

Courlander, Harold, *Negro Folk Music U.S.A.*, New York: Columbia University Press, 1963.

Ferris, William, *Blues From the Delta*, New York: Anchor Press, 1978.

Godrich, John, and Dixon, Robert, eds., *Blues and Gospel Records 1902 - 1942*, Storyville Publications, 1969.

Keil Charles, *Urban Blues*, Chicago: University of Chicago, 1966.

Kemble, Frances Anne, *Journal of a Residence on a Georgian Plantation in 1838 - 1839*, New York: Knopf, 1961.

Leadbitter, Mike, and Slaven, Neil, *Blues Records*, London: Hanover Books, 1968.

Murray, Albert, *Stomping the Blues,* New York: McGraw-Hill, 1976.

Neff, Robert, and Connor, Anthony, *Blues,* Boston: Godine, 1975.

Oliver, Paul, *The Meaning of the Blues*, New York: Collier, 1960.

Oliver, Paul, *Conversation with the Blues*, New York: Horizon Press, 1965.

Oliver, Paul, *Savannah Syncopators: African Retentions in the Blues*, New York: Stein and Day, 1970.

Oliver, Paul, *The Blues Tradition*, New York: Oak, 1968.

Oliver, Paul, *The Story of the Blues*, Philadelphia: Chilton, 1969.

Parelis, John, and Romanowski, Patricia, eds., *The Rolling Stone Encyclopedia of Rock and Roll*, New York: Rolling Stone Press, 1976.

Roach, Hildred, *Black American Music*, Boston: Crescendo, 1973.

Roberts, John Storm, *Black Music of Two Worlds*, New York: Morrow, 1974.

Rublowsky, John, *Black Music in America*, New York: Basic Books, 1971.

Shaw, Arnold, *Honkers and Shouters*, New York: Macmillan, 1978.

Southern, Eileen, *The Music of Black Americans*, New York: Norton, 1971.

Southern, Eileen, ed., *Readings in Black American Music*, New York: Norton, 1971.

Titon, Jeff Todd, *Early Downhome Blues*, Urbana: University of Illinois Press, 1977.

Writers Program of Virginia, *The Negro in Virginia*, New York: Publishers Company, 1967.